LEARN TO USE
BOOKS AND LIBRARIES

PROGRAMMED TEXTS IN
LIBRARY AND INFORMATION SCIENCE

An introduction to colon classification
 by C D Batty BA FLA

An introduction to the Dewey decimal classification
 by C D Batty BA FLA

An introduction to Sears list of subject headings
 by Philip Corrigan FLA

An introduction to the universal decimal classification
 by J M Perreault

SERIES EDITOR
C D BATTY BA FLA

LEARN TO USE
BOOKS AND LIBRARIES

A PROGRAMMED TEXT BY

T W BURRELL
FLA

CLIVE BINGLEY LONDON

FIRST PUBLISHED 1969 BY CLIVE BINGLEY LTD
16 PEMBRIDGE ROAD LONDON W11
SET IN 11 ON 13 POINT LINOTYPE PLANTIN
AND PRINTED IN GREAT BRITAIN BY
THE CENTRAL PRESS (ABERDEEN) LTD
COPYRIGHT © T W BURRELL 1969 ALL RIGHTS RESERVED
85157 076 3

CONTENTS

INTRODUCTION

This book is designed to teach you a *basic skill* which is now widely recognized as a passport to a fuller and richer personal and community life.

It is important that everyone in our society should *understand the use of books and libraries.* In *this* book:

Part 1 (*frames 1-41*) tells you *why.*

Part 2 (*frames 42-95*) tells you *what* librarians do.

Part 3 (frames 96-168) tells you *how* libraries work.

Part 4 (frames 169-248) tells you *how* to use them.

Notice that we refer to ' frame ' numbers, rather than ' page ' numbers. *This* book is not arranged like an ordinary reading book—it is a *programmed text.*

The great advantage of this form of presentation is that you will be *teaching yourself* and *testing yourself* as you go along at your own pace. Remember that:

Frame 1 is at the top of page 1.

Frame 2 is at the top of page 2.

Frame 3 is at the top of page 3, and so on.

Do *not* read a complete page at a time. At the end of frame 1 for example, ' PTO FRAME 2 ' means ' PLEASE TURN TO FRAME 2 '.

So start at frame 1, *read* the short text slowly and carefully; *respond* by answering the question marked *; *check* your answer when you ' PTO FRAME 2 '—that is when you turn to frame 2 on page 2—and then *do exactly as you are requested there*— even if the book suggests, for example, that you may ' leave out the next six frames '.

Work through the book in this way for, say, an hour at a time, or do one part at a time.

If you wish to write anything down, or *if the book tells you to make a brief written answer to a question,* do this on a *separate sheet of paper* and put the frame number against each written answer.

Correct your answers, if necessary, as indicated in the frame 'following each question, and *keep this sheet as a summary of your study* until you have really absorbed all the ideas in the programme.

You will find it easy to cheat! But remember that you are now *teaching yourself* and *testing yourself*—so if you cheat you are only *cheating yourself* and you won't learn anything that way! You may, if you wish, use the ' mask ' attached to the end paper at the rear of the book to conceal the answers.

Trust the book—you're not being brainwashed! You are, in fact, learning how to discover in books the many points of view on current problems, how to find the truth or the falsehood or the commonly accepted compromises where these have been recorded in print.

PTO FRAME I

---

83 c) *Special libraries* are organized
   i) For *special kinds of readers or*
   ii) For a *special group of readers or*
   iii) To cover *special subjects or*
   iv) To stock *special kinds of communication media*

PTO FRAME 84

---

166 Answers (based on suggestions in *frames 158-164*):
   1 Assoc Metal Workers' Soc
   2 Assoc (of) Scottish Secondary Teachers
   3 Gwynn-Williams, D
   4 Saint Patrick
   5 Saintbury, H
   6 Technology, Ministry of
   7 Willys, *Sir* Edmund
   8 Wootton of Abinger, Barbara Wright, 1st Baroness
   9 WHO

Other answers are not necessarily *wrong*.   PTO FRAME 167

1*

1 This text describes *books and libraries*. These are both very important parts of our system of *communication*.

* Do you know what this word *really* means? Even if you think you do, write down a short definition, *on your answer sheet*

PTO FRAME 2 TO CHECK ANSWER

---

84 * To which of the categories i-iv on *frame 83* do you think the following *special libraries* probably belong? Write your answers on your answer sheet alongside these names and head them ' *Special libraries* '

   i) National Film Library . . .

   ii) College libraries in general . . .

   iii) *Your* college library . . .

   iv) Science Museum Library . . .

PTO FRAME 85

---

167 * To sum up part 3, copy the following paragraph on to your answer sheet, supplying the missing words:

' Most libraries ask new readers to complete an a——for m——form. They agree to keep the simple——for the convenience of the other library users. L——a——record and control the l——of b——. An a——t of books by their s——ts is most useful to a majority of —— and this is achieved by the use of a special c——n and its associated n——n.'

PTO FRAME 168 TO CHECK ANSWER

2 We must distinguish between:

a) *Communications,* in the narrow senses of:

i) the *means of passing brief messages* such as the telephone system; *or*

ii) the *brief messages* themselves—for example, telephone conversations;

and:

PTO FRAME 3

---

85 *Special libraries*:

i) National Film Library—to stock a special kind of communication medium—film.

ii) College libraries in general—for a special kind of reader—students and teachers.

iii) *Your* college library—for a particular group of readers, in *your* college.

iv) Science Museum Library—to cover a special subject—science.

All right? If not, don't worry! PTO FRAME 86

---

168 Your summary should read:

' Most libraries ask new readers to complete an *application for membership* form. They agree to keep the simple *rules* for the convenience of the other library users. *Library assistants* record and control the *loan* of *books*. An *arrangement* of books by their *subjects* is most useful to a majority of *readers* and this is achieved by the use of a special *classification* and its associated *notation*.'

GO ON TO PART 4 (FRAME 169) WHEN YOU ARE READY

3 b) *Communication,* which may be described briefly as the *art and science of passing knowledge.*

This is the real answer to the question on *frame 1.* Correct your answer if necessary and then:

PTO FRAME 4

If you are already aware of the nature and purposes of ' communication ',

PTO FRAME 10

---

86 Remember that some so-called ' libraries ' are not really libraries as we think of them:

(a) The *commercial subscription libraries,* which charge a small weekly rental for a book, are there to make a profit and generally deal only in books for entertainment.

(b) A *private personal library* is built up for the use of one family and may well be merely a ' status symbol ' in a stately home—perhaps a very rich but inaccessible collection.

PTO FRAME 87

PART 4
HOW TO USE BOOKS AND
LIBRARIES

4 Human society can progress only if we have an adequate grasp of the technique of *communication*. This makes it possible to share knowledge between individuals, communities and generations ...

87 Some communities, even whole countries, find their welfare and development greatly handicapped by the lack of a full range of library facilities. This is one sphere in which outside ' aid ' can produce immeasurable benefits.

169 If you haven't already worked through *frames 1-41* ' Why we should understand the use of books and libraries '; *and frames 42-95* ' What librarians do '; *and frames 96-168* ' How libraries work ';
or, if you've forgotten some of the details, read the summaries on *frames 170-172.*

Otherwise, GO STRAIGHT TO FRAME 173

5 . . . who *must cooperate* in order to prosper in an economic sense and to enrich their various cultures.

Cooperation also leads to tolerance and then to a deeper regard between people. It is a sign of maturity in individuals and nations.

Libraries are meant to support and further these ideals.

PTO FRAME 6

---

88 * In what kind of libraries would you expect to find the following items? Look at *frames 74-85* again.

   i) File of *The times* newspaper for 1801.

   ii) The latest novel by Muriel Spark.

   iii) The latest Ministry of Agriculture, Fisheries and Food pamphlet on fowl pest.

   iv) Last July's issue of a Japanese textile periodical.

   v) A very dull nineteenth century book of sermons.

   vi) A copy of an early Charlie Chaplin film.

   vii) The latest edition of *Radio handbook* by W Orr.

PTO FRAME 89 TO CHECK YOUR ANSWERS

---

170 SUMMARY OF PART I

' *Literacy* is the ability to use *communication media* for receiving and passing on to others *communications and knowledge.* We acquire this ability through the process of *education* and must learn to use it at various stages of our life for purposes of *socialization, instruction, entertainment, expression* and *research.* Perhaps the most important medium to the truly literate person is the *book.*'

If this doesn't make sense, we suggest that you read *frames 1-41* before proceeding to frame 171.

6 *Communication* must therefore take place in two 'dimensions':

a) *across space*, for: government, education; artistic, scientific and technological development; and for the maintenance of friendly relations between people; *and* ...

PTO FRAME 7

---

89 i) *National library—British Museum*. Most local public libraries would have *The times* from about 1850 only, perhaps on microfilm.

ii) Your local *public library lending department*, perhaps a branch library or travelling library.

iii) Your local *public library reference department*, the ministry will probably have a copy too!

iv) *National Lending Library for Science and Technology*— apply through your local public library or college library.

For remaining answers PTO FRAME 90

---

171 SUMMARY OF PART 2

' *Librarians* are people who *select, store, display* and *deploy books and other communication media* in *libraries*. They also *help* and *train* library users. Books, *fiction* and *non-fiction,* for *lending* and *reference,* are made available through *Public, National* and *Special* libraries which *cooperate* with each other to serve readers.'

If this doesn't make sense, we suggest that you read *frames 42-95* before proceeding to frame 172.

7 . . . b) *across time,* so knowledge can be built up or *cumulated* through many generations. Only in this way can we learn from the efforts of our ancestors and pass on this sum of knowledge, with the addition of our own discoveries, to our children.

PTO FRAME 8

---

90 v) *National library*—the *British Museum* is required to keep a copy. Your local *public library* would not have shelf-space to spare for this unless the writer were a local man, in which case it should be in the *collection of local documents.*

vi) *National Film Library.*

vii) Your *college library* or local *public library lending* or *reference department*—perhaps all three.

If you scored at least 5 out of 7, PTO FRAME 91. If not—revise *frames 74-85* first.

---

172 SUMMARY OF PART 3

' Most libraries ask new readers to complete an *application for membership* form. They agree to keep the simple *rules* for the convenience of the other library users. *Library assistants* record and control the *loan* of *books.* An *arrangement* of books by their *subjects* is most useful to a majority of *readers* and this is achieved by the use of a special *classification* and its associated *notation.*'

If this doesn't make sense, we suggest that you read *frames 96-168* before proceeding to frame *173.*

8 Without communication we could not therefore :

   i) G——

   ii) E——

   iii) D——A——S——and T——

   iv) M——F——R——

   v) C——K——

  * Copy this paragraph on to your answer sheet, supplying the missing words.

PTO FRAME 9 TO CHECK ANSWER

---

91 These many different libraries do not work in isolation : not one of them could possibly s——t, s——e, d——y or d——y all the books it is likely to need . . .

  * Supply the missing words on your answer sheet. You should remember them, but revise *frames 46-49* if necessary before you go on.

PTO FRAME 92

---

173 After reading the last 172 frames, one may be forgiven for thinking that a visit to a library is likely to be something of a nightmare—but not as bad a nightmare as trying to run one!

  Of course, we have been giving you some idea of the *librarian's problems* as well as those of the *readers*. Now let's look at some *answers* to the *readers' problems*.

PTO FRAME 174

9 Answer to question on the previous frame:

' Without *communication,* we could not therefore:

   i) *Govern*

   ii) *Educate*

   iii) *Develop Art, Science* and *Technology*

   iv) *Maintain Friendly Relations*

   v) *Cumulate Knowledge*

Correct your answer if it differs substantially from this, then

PTO FRAME 10

---

92 . . . Therefore libraries should—and do— c——e with each other in several ways.

a) There are cooperative arrangements to ensure, as far as possible, that *every* important book is bought and preserved by at least *one* library *somewhere* in the country.

PTO FRAME 93

---

174 *What are your problems, as a library user?*

Probably the most pressing ones are:

a) *To know where to find books on various subjects.*

b) *To know where to find a complete list or inventory of the library's resources.*

c) *To know how to locate any particular item of the library's stock, whatever ' clue' you may have already*—author's name, title, etc.

d) *To know what may be available elsewhere.*

PTO FRAME 175

10 The ability to understand communication and use communications is known as—

' *Literacy* '

Even this has *two meanings*:

PTO FRAME II

---

93 b) There are also cooperative arrangements to ensure that *every* important book can be seen and used by *any* library member. He is usually able to use the book in his own home or in his local library, but if the book is very rare or bulky, he may have to travel to it.

* There is no prize for supplying the missing word on *frame 92* —but please cooperate by having a guess!

PTO FRAME 94

---

175 a) *To know where to find books on various subjects*:

If you wish to find a few lines in a *book* on a particular minor subject, you look in the I—— at the back of the book.

* Complete this word on your answer sheet.

PTO FRAME 176 TO CHECK ANSWER

11 a) In a narrow sense, '*literacy*' means simply the *ability to read and write*, to interpret maps, diagrams and pictures.

b) In a wider sense, it is the *further ability to absorb knowledge from the communication system and use it* to solve personal or social problems.

PTO FRAME 12

---

94 * To sum up part 2, copy the following paragraph on to your answer sheet, supplying the missing words:

'L—— are people who s——, s——, d—— and d—— books and other communication media in l——s. They also h—— and t—— library users. Books, f—— and n—— f——, for l——g and r——e, are made available through p——c, n——l, and s——l libraries which c——e with each other to serve readers.'

PTO FRAME 95 TO CHECK ANSWERS

---

176 I*ndex*, at the back of the book, of course. The index to a book consists of entries rather like these—in alphabetical order:

Subject	Page number
Highwaymen	526
Hindenburg, Paul von	102
Hitler, Adolf	730

To find out something about Adolf Hitler, you would turn to page 730 in this particular book.

PTO FRAME 177

12 Read *frames 2 and 3* again.

A '*communication medium*' is a means of passing knowledge between people and communities.

'*Communication media*' (the plural form) is therefore another name for 'communications' (*frame 2*) and is preferred because it is less likely to be confused with 'communication'.

PTO FRAME 13

---

95 Your summary should read:

'*Librarians* are people who *select, store, display* and *deploy* books and other communication media in *libraries*. They also *help* and *train* library users. Books, *fiction* and *non-fiction*, for *lending* and *reference*, are made available through *public*, *national* and *special* libraries which *cooperate* with each other to serve readers.'

Go on to part 3, beginning on *frame 96* when you are ready.

---

177 In the same way, we provide a similar guide to the location of information about *subjects*, not in a single book, but on the whole extent of the library shelves.

This guide we call the library's S—— i——.

* Complete these two words on your answer sheet, then

PTO FRAME 178 TO CHECK ANSWER

13 So this phrase ' *communication media* ' also has two aspects :

a) The *actual equipment* used—telephones, books, periodicals (magazines, journals, etc), television sets and so on.

b) The telephone *conversations*, the *texts* of books, periodical *articles* and *advertisements*, television *programmes*—that is, the *actual words and illustrations used to pass knowledge between people.*

PTO FRAME 14

PART 3
HOW LIBRARIES WORK

---

178 The *Subject index*—it may be typed on cards which are then filed in card-index drawers, or it may be on pages in a loose-leaf folder, or in any form that enables us to add entries at any point as books on *new subjects* are added to the library.

PTO FRAME 179

14 We have now learned three important concepts:

a) *Communication* is _____

_____

b) *Literacy* is _____

_____

c) *Communication media* are _____

_____

   * Copy these sentences on to your answer sheet, supplying the missing definitions.

PTO FRAME 15 TO CHECK ANSWER

96 If you haven't already worked through *frames 1-41* 'Why we should understand the use of books and libraries', and *frames 42-95* 'What librarians do'—or if you've forgotten some of the details—read the summaries on *frames 97 and 98*.

179 It lists all the *subjects* (*not* the books) represented in the library, in alphabetical order—(see *frames 158-166* again to remind yourself about the difficulties involved here)—and directs you to each by quoting, not a page number of course, but the subject number, or 'notation' allocated to that subject. (See *frames 137-155* again if in doubt about *this*.)

PTO FRAME 180

15 a) Communication is the art and science of passing knowledge (*frame 3*).

b) *Literacy* is the ability to read and write; to absorb knowledge and use it to solve problems (*frame 11*).

c) *Communication media* are the items of equipment and the actual words and illustrations used to pass knowledge (*frame 13*).

PTO FRAME 16

---

97 SUMMARY OF PART I
' *Literacy* is the ability to use *communication media* for receiving and passing on to others *communications and knowledge*. We acquire this ability through the process of *education* and must learn to use it at various stages of our life for purposes of *socialization, instruction, entertainment, expression* and *research*. Perhaps the most important medium to the truly literate person is the *book*.'

If this doesn't make sense to you, read *frames 1-41* before going on to *frame 98*.

---

180 It is this *notation,* you may remember, which—
—*determines the position of the books on the library shelves.*

PTO FRAME 181

16 If your answers differed in any important respects from those offered in *frame 15,* revise the relevant frame(s) and

PTO FRAME 17

If your answers were substantially correct

PTO FRAME 19

---

98 SUMMARY OF PART 2

' *Librarians* are people who *select, store, display* and *deploy books and other communication media* in *libraries.* They also *help* and *train* library users. Books, *fiction* and *non-fiction,* for *lending* and *reference,* are made available through *public, national* and *special* libraries which *cooperate* with each other to serve readers.'

If this doesn't make sense to you, read *frames 42-95* before going on to *frame 99.*

---

181 A section of a typical library *subject index* would look like this:

Sheet metal work	621·74
Shelley, poet	821 S
Ship building	629·12
Shoddy (textiles)	677·3
Shoe-making	685·3

Let's see how you would locate the books on, say, *sheet metal work* . . . PTO FRAME 182

17 * Complete on your answer sheet, the missing words in the following statement:

'The effectiveness of —— in passing ideas and information between people or groups, depends entirely upon the —— of the individuals concerned, that is, upon their ability to interpret and use the —— employed.'

PTO FRAME 18 TO CHECK ANSWER

99 To *join a library,* go to the *counter* just inside the entrance.

The *library assistant on duty* there will tell you whether or not you are entitled to use the library:

—do you *live in the area* served by the library?

—do you *belong to the group* served by the library?

Hardly anyone in this country is beyond the reach of some library service somewhere.

PTO FRAME 100

182 The *Subject index,* in its card index drawers or loose-leaf books, is usually kept just inside the library entrance doors.

You have looked up 'sheet metal work' in the drawer or loose-leaf book marked 'S', and have found the notation:

621·74

Where now?

PTO FRAME 183

18 The statement should read:

'The effectiveness of *communication* in passing ideas and information between people or groups, depends entirely upon the *literacy* of the individuals concerned, that is, upon their ability to interpret and use the *communication media* employed.'

No doubt you have the correct answer this time, so now

PTO FRAME 19

---

100 Look at *frame 101*—here you will find the *application-for-membership* form which you would be asked to fill in when joining a typical *college library*.

* Write on your answer sheet the details which you would have to supply—not many, are there? Then

PTO FRAME 102

---

183 Here is a plan of a typical library, and of your route in search of ' 621·74 Sheet metal work.'

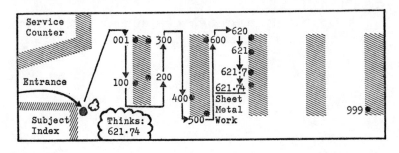

PTO FRAME 184

19 Communication media may either:

a) *Deliver a short message with considerable force*—for example, a half-hour television documentary programme on the Antarctic may leave no lasting record in the mind in spite of great initial impact. The impression is *transient in nature* and/or *limited in the extent of its coverage of the subject;* or

b) *Provide a more comprehensive and lasting record of a larger area of knowledge;* this is perhaps more important in the long run.

PTO FRAME 20

101

COLLEGE OF LIBRARY | TECHNOLOGY		
Surname		Admission No.
Forenames		
Address		
Course		
I hereby apply for membership of the College Library. I undertake to observe the rules, and to pay for any book loaned to me which is lost, seriously damaged or not returned. Date.................... Signature........................		

---

184 b) *To know where to find a complete list or inventory of the library's resources* is an important factor in exploiting these resources to the full.

The librarian also needs such a list in order to expand and control his stock of books effectively.

PTO FRAME 185

20 * On your answer sheet, rearrange the following list of *communication media* into two groups:

a) *Brief and transient*

b) *More comprehensive and lasting*

as defined on the previous frame:

Television programmes, conversations, books, films and plays, records and tapes, periodicals and newspapers, radio programmes, paintings and drawings, sculpture, lectures.

PTO FRAME 21 TO CHECK YOUR LISTS

---

102 Look at *frames 103 and 104*—here you will find the front and back of the *application-for-membership form* which you would be asked to fill in when joining a typical *public library*.

* Write on your answer sheet the details which you would have to supply. Then

PTO FRAME 105

---

185 This inventory or list of stock is known in libraries as a ' *Catalogue* '—the word is also well known in the retail trade and especially in other parts of the book trade.

This catalogue, although also probably in card or loose-leaf form, lists *not* the subjects represented in the library (this is the job of the subject index—see *frame 179*), *but the actual books themselves* ...

PTO FRAME 186

21 a) *Brief and transient*
Television programmes
Conversations
Films and plays
Records and tapes
Periodicals & newspapers
Radio programmes
Paintings & drawings
Sculpture
Lectures

b) *Comprehensive, lasting*
Books,

but:
Some of the items in Group a) can be kept for a short time by recording them on film, tape or records

PTO FRAME 22

103

```
------------ PUBLIC  LIBRARIES
            Application for reader's tickets

   Mr.
I  Mrs.   ( Name in full )
 , Miss.  ( Block letters )  ...................................................................

living at................................................................................full postal address
Apply for tickets to borrow books in accordance with the rules and regulations which I
agree to observe.

Age (if under 21) ...............................

Date................................       Signature.................................................................

Business Address (or School)
if not resident in ---------   ........................................................................

R 61302              Please write in ink and do not fold this card
```

186 . . . *in the order in which they stand on the shelves.* ie according to their various subjects, hence we call this the *subject catalogue.*

i) It is a *complete and easily accessible list of the library's resources* on any subject.

ii) It therefore *lists items which are not on the shelves when we visit the library*—some may be on loan to other readers; many, such as films and records, are stored elsewhere than on the bookshelves.

PTO FRAME 187

22 The lesson that you should have learned from this exercise is that a *book* is virtually the only communication medium that is:

i) *Able to deal comprehensively with a large area of knowledge.*

In addition it is:

ii) *A more or less permanent record.*

iii) *Relatively cheap to buy.*

iv) *Convenient to store.*

v) *Convenient to use anywhere at any time.*

PTO FRAME 23

104

GUARANTEE

This side need be filled in, only if the applicant's name does not appear in the current register of electors.

I Mr.
Mrs. (Name in full)
Miss. (Block letters) ....

living at.:...:...full postal address

being a registered elector in the County Borough of ━━━━━━ recommend the applicant named overleaf as a person to whom books may be safely entrusted and hereby undertake in default of the applicant, to replace or pay the value of any books lost or damaged by the applicant, also to·pay all fines and expenses incurred in the recovery of any book; it being agreed that the liability shall not exceed forty shillings.

Date..   Signature..

---

187 A typical *Subject catalogue ' entry '* would look like this:

```
621·396
    ORR, William I
        Radio handbook; 17th edition
        Foulsham - Sams, 1967.
        848 p. illus., plans, tables.
```

PTO FRAME 188

23 *But* a book can also share some of the best features of other communication media:

vi) It can be *illustrated* by photographs, maps, etc.

vii) Its message can be *supplemented by other media,* for example, an accompanying filmstrip.

viii) It can be *kept up-to-date* by the issue of new editions.

ix) An index will *analyse* small items of information in the text.

PTO FRAME 24

---

105 Note that in *this* case, the *public library* asks for your *age* because:

a) If you were younger than about 15 years, you would be referred to the *junior library.*

b) Unless you were over 21 years, and therefore on the official list of voters in your district, you would be asked to find an older person, a *relative or friend, to support your application.*

PTO FRAME 106

---

188 Notice that, although we cannot put a book in two different places on the shelves where it might be useful, *we can put an extra card in the subject catalogue,* for example, at 621·396 Radio, to tell a reader looking through the entries that there is a book, shelved at 537 Physics: theoretical electricity, which might be of use to him. This card is called an ' *Added entry* ' and gives all the important details of the physics book in the form shown on the previous frame.

PTO FRAME 189

24 *To summarize frames 22 and 23,* we can say that:

Books are usually—*comprehensive, permanent, cheap, convenient.*

Books can be—*illustrated, supplemented, up-dated, analysed.*

It is often found necessary to *supplement other media,* for example, a film or a set of records, by a *printed text or commentary* in book form.

PTO FRAME 25

---

106 Note also:

c) In neither library is there any *charge* for joining or using the books, although you may have to pay to borrow records, or to replace books which you may lose or damage.

d) Your signature really indicates that you agree to obey the *rules* of the library.

PTO FRAME 107

---

189 * To refresh your memory on the last fourteen frames, write on your answer sheets the words missing from the following summary:

' At the back of most books, an —— helps you to find references to the various —— mentioned in the text. It lists these in —— order and refers to them by p—— n——. A library's S—— I—— guides you to the location of books on various —— on the library's ——. Instead of page numbers, it uses the —— to describe where a subject is to be found.'

PTO FRAME 190

25 * Copy out these sentences on to your answer sheet, supplying the missing words :

Books are usually c—— p—— c—— c——

Books can be i—— s—— u—— a——

PTO FRAME 26

---

107 The *library rules* are usually displayed, or are printed as a label to be pasted into each book. The rules are kept to a minimum and are meant to ensure that everyone, including yourself, has a fair opportunity to use the library and its books and other resources, without being disturbed or frustrated. This is your *right* once you become a member, but . . .

PTO FRAME 108

---

190 * The library's inventory or list of books is known as the S—— c—— because : *entries are arranged* . . . ——————

Its main functions are to present :

i) *A complete and easily accessible inventory of* . . . ——

ii) *A list of those items which* . . . ———————————

PTO FRAME 191

34

26 Sure you got those right?

Check your answers on *frame 24*.

WHEN SATISFIED PTO FRAME 27

---

108 . . . people who acquire rights also acquire the *obligation to respect the rights of other people.*

* Write down on your answer sheet *four* rules which you think any library could reasonably ask its members to obey.

PTO FRAME 109 TO CHECK ANSWERS

---

191 The missing words, in order, are:

Index, subjects, alphabetical, page numbers, subject index, subjects, shelves, notation.

Subject catalogue. 'Entries are arranged in the same subject order as are the books on the shelves.'

i) *'A complete and easily accessible list of the library's resources on any subject.'*

ii) *'A list of those items which are not on the shelves when we visit the library.'*

PTO FRAME 192

27 *Without good communications* across space and time, especially in the form of *books,* we should still be in the same condition as some of the following peoples: Australian aborigines, Germans, Red Indians, Japanese, Stone Age men, atomic scientists, Russians, poets, Tibetans, Hottentots—have inadequate *communications* and so find *communication* difficult or impossible.

* *Which? —write your selection on your answer sheet.*

PTO FRAME 28 TO CHECK ANSWER

---

109 *Perm any four from this list of rules:*

i) People should give full and correct details when filling in application-for-membership forms.

ii) They should not take out books to which they are not entitled.

iii) They should return books on or before the due date.

iv) They should report any change of home address.

v) They should report any case of infectious disease at home, although books do *not* normally carry infection.

vi) They should never disturb or offend other readers.

PTO FRAME 110

---

192 * Have another look at *frame 187* and then try to write out a subject catalogue entry for the following book. Lay out your entry in an oblong 5 in long by 3 in wide on your answer sheet —this is the size of a normal catalogue card.

' *A shorter European history 1756-1943* ' by George W Southgate, published by J M Dent and Sons Ltd in 1944. It has 285 pages, and is kept at subject number 940.

PTO FRAME 193 TO CHECK ANSWER

28 Your selection should read:

Australian aborigines, Red Indians, Stone Age men, Tibetans, Hottentots (from SW Africa).

These people have no technologies and no comforts—the Stone Age men haven't even survived!

They have never been educated to receive or pass on knowledge except through their own very limited tribal traditions and experience. They are not literate. If still in doubt, *see frames 10 and 11*. Then

PTO FRAME 29

---

110 So much for application forms and rules!
—How do we get books out of this place?

Different libraries have different methods of *recording the loan of books* to their readers, but most methods involve the combining at the *service counter* of one of your *reader's tickets*, bearing your name and address, and a *book-card* bearing details to identify the book which you wish to take out. *So don't forget to call at the counter* on the way out.

PTO FRAME 111

---

193 This is how we would enter the details of Southgate's book in the subject catalogue:

```
940
     SOUTHGATE, George W
         Shorter European History 1756-1943
         Dent, 1944
         285 p.
```

PTO FRAME 194

29 *Communication media must be used with a high sense of responsibility to the community* in which they are employed.

A dictator, or even the sponsor of a commercial television programme, will try to gain control of books and broadcasting and turn them to his own purposes so that unthinking people will be deceived by the media which they are accustomed to trust.

No test on this! So

PTO FRAME 30

---

111 At the same time, a record is made of the date by which you should have returned the book to the library—two or three weeks are usually allowed for reading.

Try to bring the book back before this date, so that it is available for any other reader who may be waiting for it (see *frame 109*).

PTO FRAME 112

---

194 If you feel that you now understand clearly the difference between the

Subject index and the *Subject catalogue*

PTO FRAME 195

If not:

REVISE FRAMES 175-188
[* *In any case: Go to a library* at the first convenient opportunity to look at these ' guides ' to the stock.]

30 We saw in *frame 28* that people who are not *literate* are unable to communicate fully.

They are therefore unable to give *help to others,* or make effective use of *help offered to them by others.*

The name given to the process by which people can be made literate is E——.

* Copy this sentence on to your answer sheet, supplying the missing word.

PTO FRAME 31 TO CHECK ANSWER

---

112 If you *do* keep your book past the ' date due back ' without asking to have the loan *renewed,* don't be surprised or offended if your library sends you a ' *reminder* ' *postcard* and charges you for the inconvenience you cause.

[But, of course, *you* wouldn't do this, would you?]

PTO FRAME 113

---

195 c) Many readers come into a library, not just to ' look at a few books ' on a particular subject, say, Radio at 621·396, but *to locate one particular book* on Radio—perhaps :

Radio handbook 17th edition, by William Orr.

They may have been recommended to read this book by an instructor or a friend, or may have seen it reviewed—*and no other will do.*

PTO FRAME 196

31 The word is *Education.*

This began when you were still a baby in the family group at home.

You were taught to *survive* and to *tolerate others.* This is known as '*socialization*' and is strictly non-political at this stage!

PTO FRAME 32

---

113 We have already said (frames 44-51) that *librarians* are people who are trained to *select, store, display* and *deploy books* and to *help people to state their needs clearly and carry out the first stages of the search themselves.*

Library assistants, on the other hand, are not professionally qualified librarians (although they may qualify later after studying) but they have very important jobs.

PTO FRAME 114

---

196 How can our readers find out whether or not the library has this particular book?

i) They could, of course, look in the *Subject index,* see that books on radio are at number 621·396 and search the shelves there, but the book might quite possibly be out on loan to another reader.

ii) They could, instead, look in the *Subject catalogue* at this number and search through all the cards on various aspects of radio, but this would take a long time—and suppose that we had 'classed' this book at 534·86 as a physics book!

PTO FRAME 197

32 Later you were taught to read and write and observe, so that the various communication media could be used for your *instruction*—in the techniques of *learning* and *earning*.

This is probably still going on.

PTO FRAME 33

---

114 The *Library assistant's work* includes:

a) Carrying out the counter routines of lending and receiving back books; recalling books which are overdue from loan; enrolling new members.

b) Helping new readers to find their way about.

c) Advising some readers on their choice of books.

d) Displaying and safeguarding the collections.

e) Helping in all ways to maintain friendly relations with readers and non-readers alike throughout the community.

PTO FRAME 115

---

197 It seems that there is a need for a *third* ' library guide '—another list or catalogue, rather like the subject catalogue, but arranged to help us to find in the library a book which the reader knows by the author's name, or the title, or even by the name of the artist or photographer who illustrated it, the editor who put together the work of several contributors, the firm or society which sponsored it, or the series to which it belongs.

PTO FRAME 198

33 There comes a time at which you find that the same media will bring you

Entertainment

and later still, you may discover that you can use these media for the

Expression of your own ideas and personality to instruct or entertain others.

PTO FRAME 34

---

115 * Copy these questions on to your sheet and add the answers:

Should you ask the Library assistant to:

a) Show you how to fill in the application-for-membership form?

b) Show you how to find the books on radio servicing?

c) Order five very expensive books on radio servicing for the library stock?

d) Change the library rules about the length of time you can keep a book?

e) Go out with you after work?

PTO FRAME 116

---

198 Since these are all names, words, they can be arranged in a catalogue in the familiar *alphabetical order,* using as many cards or loose-leaf entries for each book as may be necessary to cover all the names by which readers might recognize, remember and request it. This single big alphabetical catalogue is usually called the *Name catalogue* and the entries are almost identical with that shown on *frame 187* for the subject catalogue. Have another look at this, then

PTO FRAME 199

34 One important aim of your teachers *now* is to ensure that at all times you use the media freely for your own purposes of

Research and enquiry

when trying to keep your knowledge of your own particular interests up to date, and also when investigating new fields of interest.

PTO FRAME 35

---

116 You should have answers on the following lines:

a) *Yes*—but the librarian should make his forms easy to fill in—they need not be complicated.

b) *Yes*—but she should show you the guide which helps you to locate books on *any* subject rather than just lead you to the radio books on the shelves.

c) *No*—the librarian is responsible for book selection.

d) *No*—even the librarian would consult the Library Committee about changing the rules.

e) This might come under the heading of ' friendly relations ' (see *frame 114 e*).

PTO FRAME 117

---

199 We have already considered some of the difficulties of arranging *books* in alphabetical order (*frames 158-166*)—but in the name catalogue we are arranging cards.

Take the example of William SMITH-DAVIES (*frame 160*).

We should probably put our main card, as suggested, at ' SMITH-DAVIES, William '. But we can also put another card, ' *added entry* ', under ' D ' at ' DAVIES, William SMITH-' or, we could put instead a simple ' *cross-reference* ' ' DAVIES, *William* SMITH—*see* SMITH-DAVIES, *William* '.

PTO FRAME 200

35 At this stage of your career, you should be a '*Master of the media*'—you will have learned to look at them critically and to use them for :

    * S————.

      I————.

      E————.

      E————.

      R————.

Complete these key words on your answer sheet, then

PTO FRAME 36 TO CHECK ANSWERS

---

117 It is time that we looked at the *arrangement of books in the library*. So far (*frame 55*), we have spoken only of a ' useful arrangement '—useful *to whom?*—and *for what?*

PTO FRAME 118

---

200 * List on your answer sheet at least four of the many kinds of name which may appear at the head of a n—— c—— card :

   i) A————R

  ii) I ————R

 iii) S————R

 iv) E————R

  v) T————E

 vi) S————S

Why should readers take the trouble to discover and remember these details about a book which they are likely to need from a library or bookshop?

PTO FRAME 201

36 You should have written the key words:

Socialization
Instruction
Entertainment
Expression
Research

If you did *not* write all these, go back and read *frames 31-34* again. If you were correct

PTO FRAME 37

---

118 Assuming that readers are to have access to the library shelves, as is the case in most libraries, the arrangement of books should be:

Useful to the readers (not primarily to the librarians!).
in the sense that it should be made as easy as possible for readers to find the books which they need.

PTO FRAME 119

---

201 These *kinds of names* may be used at the head of a name catalogue card:

i) *AUTHOR*
ii) *ILLUSTRATOR*
iii) *SPONSOR*
iv) *EDITOR*
v) *TITLE*
vi) *SERIES*

Readers will find that by remembering these details and looking for them in the library's name catalogue they can very quickly identify and locate the books they need.

PTO FRAME 202

37 *Why is this important to you?*

Assuming that you have recently started work or will soon be looking for your first job, your working life should last about 45 years.

During that time, society and work will change so completely that *you may have to re-learn the theory and practice of your job and other activities several times over,* even if you never change your work or win promotion to other functions—*but . . .*

PTO FRAME 38

---

119 What methods of book arrangement can you think of?
   * Make a list on your answer sheet, and then

PTO FRAME 120

---

202 Books and other items which are in the stock of your library and are therefore listed in the subject catalogue and in the name catalogue, may be either :

   i) *Found on the shelves* at the appropriate subject number.

   ii) *Obtained from the assistant* at the counter if kept in some other part of the library, *or*

   iii) *Reserved for you* if not immediately available.

PTO FRAME 203

38 . . . colleges will be too crowded with new entrants to offer normal type 'refresher courses'. *You will therefore probably be expected to re-socialize and instruct yourself* to a large extent, by reading, watching selected television programmes, writing answers to questions posted to you by tutors you have never seen and using self-instructional programmed texts like this one.

If you don't *retrain,* you'll be *redundant.*

PTO FRAME 39

---

120 How about arranging your books:

a) *By author's name?* Many people have favourite authors and ask regularly for their books.

b) *By size?* This would economize in shelf-space, but what is the size of *your* favourite book? In any case, eighty percent of books are 8in. × 5in. × 1½in.

c) *By colour?* A new idea for interior decorators, perhaps. but not very efficient for our purpose.

d) *By title?* This could work well if everyone knew the exact title of the book required.

PTO FRAME 121

---

203 d) *But perhaps your library does not have the items you require*—well, you have already learned about the ways in which libraries cooperate with each other to obtain books which are not commonly available. (If you don't remember much about this, revise *frames 91-93.) How can we discover what is available elsewhere?*

Suppose, further, that you have no particular author or title in mind *so that you don't know what to ask for.*

PTO FRAME 204

39 This is one important reason why you must ' *master the media* '—but don't forget the other important purposes of communication :

Entertainment.

Expression of your own ideas and personality.

Research and enquiry.

These are very important to our way of life and make the ' rat-race ' worthwhile!

PTO FRAME 40

---

121 Names, size, colour—if we all noticed and remembered these details every time, the police would have a comparatively easy time identifying suspects from witnesses' descriptions—so would librarians.

* Most readers don't remember—or never knew—such details about the books they want—but they all know the *subjects* in which they are interested for the time being, so we must try to ————————————. Complete this sentence on your answer sheet.

PTO FRAME 122 TO CHECK ANSWER

---

204 It is extremely useful to know how to trace books and articles which are in existence, even if not stocked in your own library, since it is usually possible to borrow them in limited numbers for short periods if they are essential to your work or study.

Of course, if they are available, and suitable, for purchase, your librarian may be prepared to buy them for the library.

PTO FRAME 205

40 * To sum up part 1, copy out the following paragraph on to your answer sheet, supplying the missing words:

' L—— is the ability to use c—— m—— for receiving and passing on to others c——s and k——. We acquire this ability through the process of e—— and must learn to use it at various stages of our life for purposes of s——, i——, e——, e——, and r——. Perhaps the most important medium to the truly literate person is the b——.'

PTO FRAME 41 TO CHECK ANSWER

---

122 *We must try to arrange books by their subjects.*
Easier said than done—could we use alphabetical order? For example:

Abattoirs	—but we could	*Slaughterhouses*
Abbeys	choose other	*Monasteries*
Abbreviations	words that mean	*Contractions*
Abdications	the same :—	*Resignations.*

These names, if chosen, would place the books on these subjects in a quite different order and how would our readers know which name to look for?

PTO FRAME 123

---

205 i) Firstly, there are *bibliographies*. These are very valuable publications which aim to *list all the books*:
Published in a given country and/or period.
For example:

The *British national bibliography* is published every week and lists all the books published in Great Britain during the preceding week, by their subjects (using the Dewey decimal library classification) and by their authors and titles.

PTO FRAME 206

41 Your summary should read:

' *Literacy* is the ability to use *communication media* for receiving and passing on to others *communications* and *knowledge*. We acquire this ability through the process of *education* and must learn to use it at various stages of our life for purposes of *socialization, instruction, entertainment, expression* and *research*. Perhaps the most important medium to the truly literate person is the *book*.'

Go on to Part 2, beginning on FRAME 42, when you are ready.

---

123 *Further*:

Why separate books on *Abattoirs* from other books on the *Meat trade*?

or collections of books on *Abbeys* from other books on, say, *Architecture* and *Church history*?

and so on.

Alphabetical order of subjects doesn't seem very efficient, or consistent either.

PTO FRAME 124

---

206 Other types of *bibliographies* aim to *list all the books*:

Published on a given subject, or by a given writer.

There is even a well-known

Bibliography of bibliographies—sort that one out!

Note that the ' bibliographies ' which you often find in textbooks are usually *short reading lists*, but although they are not comprehensive, they can be very useful in suggesting further reading.

PTO FRAME 207

PART 2

WHAT LIBRARIANS DO

124 Many people have tried to solve this problem of arranging books in order by their *subjects*.

Few successful schemes have emerged, but they all have this in common—they are all based on the idea of a *family tree* —a chart showing the different generations or stages in the development of a family and the relationship of the various members.

PTO FRAME 125

207 ii) *Periodical indexes* list periodical articles just as bibliographies list books. They aim to *list all the useful periodical articles published within a given country and/or period* and usually arrange them *in order by their subjects*.

For example :
between them the *British technology index* and the *British humanities index* analyse nearly 600 periodicals monthly and quarterly respectively, and cover the whole field of knowledge as listed on *frame 136*.

PTO FRAME 208

42 If you haven't already worked through *frames 1-41* ' Why we should understand the use of books and libraries ', or if you've forgotten some of the details, read the summary on *frame 43*.

Otherwise

GO STRAIGHT TO FRAME 44

---

125 For example:

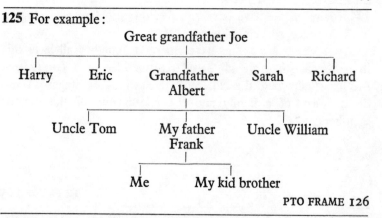

PTO FRAME 126

---

208 iii) *Periodical abstracts* go still further and give us a brief summary of each article listed. These naturally take rather longer to prepare for publication, but are extremely valuable in helping you to decide whether or not to ask for the complete article, or may even be an adequate substitute for it. *Technical education abstracts* is a good example of this kind of service, but there are many more dealing regularly with up to date developments in many subjects.

PTO FRAME 209

'*Literacy* is the ability to use *communication media* for receiving and passing on to others *communications and knowledge*. We acquire this ability through the process of *education* and must learn to use it at various stages of our life for purposes of *socialization, instruction, entertainment, expression* and *research*. Perhaps the most important medium to the truly literate person is the *book*.'

If this doesn't make sense to you, read *frames 1-41* before going on to *frame 44*.

---

126 Apply this idea to all the subjects about which books have been written—for example, take the *sciences*:

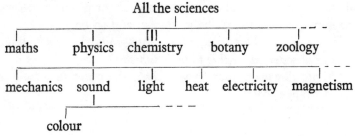

All the sciences

PTO FRAME 127

---

209 * Copy out the following paragraph on to your answer sheet, supplying the missing words:

'P—— i—— and p—— a—— list important —— ——, usually in s—— order, at monthly or quarterly intervals. On the other hand, b—— list b—— published in a given c——y and/or p——, or on a given s—— or by a given a——.'

PTO FRAME 210

44 *Librarians* undertake professional training which helps them to:

PTO FRAME 45

---

127 Imagine that one book was written about each of the subjects listed on *frame 126* (forgotten?—have another look!); one about all the sciences, one about maths, one about physics, one each about mechanics, sound, light, colour, and so on.

How could we best arrange these thirteen books on a bookshelf in a useful order, according to their subjects?

* Write down on your answer sheet the order in which *you* would arrange them.

PTO FRAME 128 TO CHECK ANSWER

---

210 You should have the following summary on your answer sheet:

'*Periodical indexes* and *periodical abstracts* list important *magazine articles,* usually in *subject* order, at monthly or quarterly intervals. On the other hand, *bibliographies* list *books* published in a given *country* and/or *period* or on a given *subject* or by a given *author.*'

Any errors? If so recheck *frames 203-208.*

PTO FRAME 211

45 *Select*
   Store

   Display
   Deploy

all kinds of information
and knowledge—
(' *Communication* '—remember?)
—for a particular group or
organization or community.

PTO FRAME 46

128 How about this?

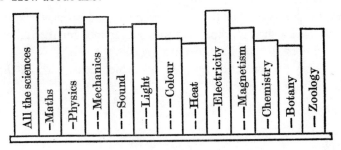

PTO FRAME 129

211 If you feel rather confused after the previous thirty frames, *frame 212,* which is a repeat of an earlier frame, *174,* lists again the problems which confront most regular library users most of the time.

PTO FRAME 212

46 *Selection*: is necessary because the output of books alone amounts to 25,000 *separate titles* each year in this country.

Perhaps one third of these are rubbish, another third unsuitable for our particular library—and we can, perhaps, afford to buy only one third of the remainder anyway!

PTO FRAME 47

---

129 Notice that by this arrangement:

a) All the books on the sciences are together on one section of the library shelves, separated into subsections for the different sciences—*maths, physics, chemistry, botany, zoology.*

b) They are preceded by the book which deals with *all these sciences together.* Further . . .

PTO FRAME 130

---

212 Probably the most pressing problems are:

a) *To know where to find books on various subjects.*

b) *To know where to find a complete list or inventory of the library's resources.*

c) *To know how to locate any particular item of the library's stock, whatever 'clue' you may have already—title, author's name, etc.*

d) *To know how to find out what may be available in other libraries.*

PTO FRAME 213

47 *Storage*: can be a great problem—few storekeepers in industry have to look after, literally, fifty or more miles of shelves, containing several millions of individual items, hundreds of packed filing cabinets and lists or inventories with many millions of entries.

There are many libraries of this magnitude and they are growing in size day by day.

PTO FRAME 48

---

130 . . . c) The book on each science is followed immediately by books dealing with the *parts* of that science, as, for example,
  physics is followed by the books on
  mechanics, sound, light, heat, electricity, magnetism
and as, for example,
  light is followed by the book on *colour*.

PTO FRAME 131

---

213 Write on your answer sheet the names of the particular library guides which are designed to provide answers to the problems listed on the previous frame:

    a) ————————————————
    b) ————————————————
    c) ————————————————
    d) ————————————————

PTO FRAME 214 TO CHECK ANSWERS

48 *Display*: is vital if people are to be attracted to the collections and made aware of the range of their contents.

Big department stores make good use of this art—supermarkets could not exist without it.

PTO FRAME 49

---

131 We must remember that, besides *physics*, each of the other sciences mentioned here—*maths, chemistry, botany* and *zoology* —would be followed immediately by books on its own constituent parts, such as:

arithmetic, algebra, geometry ...

analytical, inorganic, organic, chemistry ...

and so on—hundreds of them altogether in orderly '*family groups*'.

PTO FRAME 132

---

214 a) *Subject index (frames 175-184)*
   b) *Subject catalogue (frames 184-194)*
   c) *Name catalogue (frames 195-202)*
   d) *Bibliographies,*
      periodical indexes and abstracts (frames 203-210)

BEFORE YOU PTO FRAME 215, TURN TO THE LARGE DIAGRAM ON PAGE 93 AT THE BACK OF THIS BOOK.   NOW PTO FRAME 215

49 *Deployment*: simply means ensuring that books and other resources are routed to the people who need them—and later recovered for further use by others.

PTO FRAME 50

---

132 We must also remember that, beside SCIENCE, there are other great divisions of human knowledge about which books are written.

One of the important schemes of arrangement, mentioned on *frame 134*, lists *nine* such great divisions.

PTO FRAME 133

---

215 This large diagram is a ' *flow chart* '.

This kind of diagram is used to clarify problems and suggest methods of dealing with them. Here it is used to describe:
a useful procedure for searching libraries, a procedure which you can learn, like a drill, and apply in almost any library in order to:
obtain the book or information which you need.

Follow the diagram as you work through the next twelve frames. Now

PTO FRAME 216

50 Librarians must also be prepared to *help and, perhaps, train people to*:

a) *state their needs in 'library language'*—for example: 'I need the book by William Orr entitled *Radio handbook,* 17th edition, published last year in the United States—no other book or edition will do.'

and also:

PTO FRAME 51

---

133 This scheme for arranging books by their subjects was devised by an American librarian named Melvil Dewey in 1876. It has been kept up to date by the issue of new editions to allow for the introduction into libraries of books on new subjects like 'lasers', 'hovercraft', 'Tanzania'. This scheme, or a variant of it, is used in eighty percent of libraries all over the world and in ninety percent of British libraries.

PTO FRAME 134

---

216 Firstly, it is essential that you should '*Define exactly what it is that you need*' (*point A*). For example, are you looking for:

1 *One particular book on radio,* called *Radio handbook,* by William Orr, 17th edition, 1967? If you can't find this, are you prepared to accept an alternative?

2 *A very highly specialized book* on, say, aerial systems? You've heard of one but you can't remember any details and your library may not have it in stock.

3 *Any radio book which may be available* when you call?

PTO FRAME 217

51 b) *Carry out by themselves, in the library, the first stages of the search for what they need.*

The supermarkets call this 'self-service' and libraries have been operating in this way for fifty years, so that trained *librarians* can concentrate on skilled professional work and *readers* can get to know library resources much more quickly and completely.

PTO FRAME 52

---

134 The nine great divisions or 'classes' of the Dewey classification are:

PHILOSOPHY
RELIGION
SOCIAL STUDIES
LANGUAGES
SCIENCES
TECHNOLOGIES
ARTS
LITERATURES
HISTORY & GEOGRAPHY

To these, Dewey added a tenth class to hold books which will not fit into any of these classes: Class GENERAL BOOKS comes first in the arrangement.

PTO FRAME 135

---

217 *If 1, follow the unbroken lines on the chart.* Your first call should be at the *NAME CATALOGUE 'B'* to find out whether or not the library has a copy of this book in its stock.

i) *If the book is listed in the catalogue,* the catalogue entry will direct you to the appropriate place on the *SHELVES 'E'*, where you should find it—621·396.

If it is not there on the shelves, ask the assistant at the *COUNTER 'F'* to reserve it for you when it is returned to the library.

PTO FRAME 218

52 * Copy out this summary on to your answer sheet, supplying the missing words:

' Librarians are people who:

S————,
S————,
D————,
D————,

} books and other ' media of communication '

Librarians should also h—— and t—— their readers to become efficient library users.'

PTO FRAME 53 TO CHECK ANSWER

---

135 * Can you name, on your answer sheet, one kind of book which would have to go into the first class—GENERAL BOOKS?

If you can't think of even one, look at *frame 66* for the answer —and the reasoning behind it.

' Then learn by heart the list of the main classes of the Dewey classification in the order in which they appear on

FRAME 136

---

218 *If the book you want is not listed in the catalogue* (that is, it is not in the library stock),
either ii) *look for an acceptable alternative book*
by looking in the *SUBJECT INDEX ' C '* under ' Radio ' to find the subject number 621.396, and then looking on the *SHELVES ' E '* at this number *to see whether or not an acceptable alternative book is immediately available.*

PTO FRAME 219

53 The missing words are, of course:

Select, Store, Display, Deploy, Help, Train.

If you *didn't* get these right, have another look at *frames 44-52.*

* Then try to describe briefly, on your answer sheet, the purpose of this particular programmed text as you understand it.

PTO FRAME 54 TO CHECK STATEMENT

---

136 Dewey classification

0 GENERAL BOOKS	
1 PHILOSOPHY	
2 RELIGION	
3 SOCIAL STUDIES	* Now test yourself
4 LANGUAGES	on your answer
5 SCIENCES	sheet until you
6 TECHNOLOGIES	know these by
7 ARTS	heart. Then
8 LITERATURES	
9 HISTORY & GEOGRAPHY	

PTO FRAME 137

---

219 *if no acceptable alternative is immediately available,* go back to the *SUBJECT CATALOGUE 'D'* at this same number, 621·396, to see whether or not an acceptable book or other item exists in the library's stock; if it does, ask the library assistant at the *COUNTER 'F'* to reserve it for you.

PTO FRAME 220

54 This particular programme is intended to *help and train you to become an efficient library user;* to teach you how to:

a) *State your needs in ' library language '.*

b) *Carry out, by yourself, in the library, the first stages of the search for what you need.*

PTO FRAME 55

---

137 You may already have wondered how we *mark a book with its subject* in such a way that it can be given a place in the whole arrangement and put back quickly and easily, for example, after it has been returned to the library by a reader.

Do we write ' Physics—light-colour ' across the spine of the book? Do we use shorthand or colour-coding?

PTO FRAME 138

---

220 Or: iii) *If you do not want an alternative book* ask the assistant at the *COUNTER ' F '* to consult with the librarian as to whether or not the book might be

bought for the library, or

borrowed for you from another library.

This latter course of action is not usually possible in the case of novels, new books or books costing less than about £2.

PTO FRAME 221

55 *Libraries* are buildings in which you can expect to find the *selected books* and other items, *stored* and *displayed* in a useful arrangement, with facilities for their *deployment* to *readers* who need them.

PTO FRAME 56

138 We do, in fact, use a *notation,* or ' code ' of numbers which is printed on the spine of each book *to describe its subject and location.*

Look at *frame 136* again—note that we have numbered the ten main classes from 0 to 9.

In the Dewey classification's notation, these numbers *may be expanded to three figures,* so that Philosophy becomes *100,* Religion *200* and so on.

PTO FRAME 139

221 *If 2,* (refresh your memory from *frame 216), follow the dashes on the chart.*

Your library is unlikely to stock a highly specialized ' monograph ' and perhaps you are unlikely to know much about one —or even be sure that such a work exists—on a minor subject such as ' aerial systems '. But:

i) If you *do* know any detail, such as an author's name or a title, check the *NAME CATALOGUE ' B '.*

PTO FRAME 222

56 In most libraries a high proportion of the books *may be borrowed for reading at home,* especially those books in which the information is arranged in *continuous, or narrative, form.*

PTO FRAME 57

---

139 * Now write out on your answer sheet, the *notations* for all the main classes listed on *frame 136.*

PTO FRAME 140 TO CHECK ANSWER

---

222 ii) *Even if you don't know any details,* it might be worth checking the *SUBJECT INDEX 'C'* to find the subject number for 'aerial systems'—621·396·67—so that you can search through all the cards in the *SUBJECT CATALOGUE 'D'* at that number *to see whether or not the library possesses a suitable book.*

If it does, search the *SHELVES 'E'* at that number for the book, or ask the assistant at the *COUNTER 'F'* to reserve it for you if necessary.

PTO FRAME 223

57 These books which may be borrowed for home-reading are usually divided into:

a) *Fiction,* and

b) *Non-fiction.*

Of course, you *know* the difference, but if it just won't come past the tip of your tongue, have a quick look at *frames 58-61.*

If you are *quite sure* about this distinction

PTO FRAME 62

140

000	GENERAL BOOKS	
100	PHILOSOPHY	The reason for this
200	RELIGION	three-figure basis
300	SOCIAL STUDIES	is that it helps us
400	LANGUAGES	to make up ' notations '
500	SCIENCES	for books dealing
600	TECHNOLOGIES	with thousands of
700	ARTS	*parts* or *sub-divisions*
800	LITERATURES	of these main classes—
900	HISTORY & GEOGRAPHY	

PTO FRAME 141

---

223 iii) *If the library does not possess a suitable book,* search *BIBLIOGRAPHIES ' G '*—for example:

Reading lists in radio books that are in the library.

Special bibliographies listing books on radio topics.

General bibliographies, covering all publications of the country for recent years, which are arranged in subject order or well-indexed.

Periodical indexes and abstracts which may refer to useful articles recently published in, say, *Wireless world* or *Practical wireless.*

PTO FRAME 224

58 *Fiction books* tell a story that is *not true,* although it may be based upon an actual event or involve real people—often historical characters.

It is a product of the writer's imagination and when it is written in ordinary prose it is called a ' *novel* ': it may also be in the form of *poetry* or a *play,* however.

PTO FRAME 59

141—For example, turn back to frame 126 and let us have another look at main class 500 sciences and its constituent parts : —

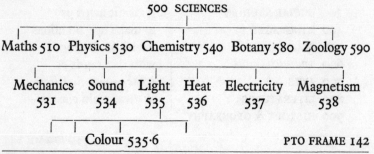

500 SCIENCES

Maths 510   Physics 530   Chemistry 540   Botany 580   Zoology 590

Mechanics 531   Sound 534   Light 535   Heat 536   Electricity 537   Magnetism 538

Colour 535·6

PTO FRAME 142

---

224 Any item identified in this way will presumably have to be:
bought for the library, or
borrowed for you from another library as in *frame 220.*

If you're not sure about the meaning of some of the terms on *frame 223,* revise *frames 204-210.* Then

PTO FRAME 225

59 *Non-fiction books* are written to describe *real* places, people, events, sciences, arts and processes.

PTO FRAME 60

---

142 Compare this 'family tree' with that on *frame 125* and note how it is possible to indicate sub-division through many 'generations' by using the decimal point.

In the Dewey classification, there can be up to *ten subdivisions* at each 'stage' or 'level' or 'generation' of every main class such as science. The numbers are read ' *decimally* '— that is, 535 precedes, 535·6 and 536 follows it in the 'family tree' and on the library shelves. Because of this, the scheme is usually referred to as the *Dewey decimal classification*.

PTO FRAME 143

---

225 *If 3* (refresh your memory from *frame 216*), *follow the dotted line on the chart.*

Look in the *SUBJECT INDEX ' C '* for the subject number —621·396—then go to search the *SHELVES ' E '* at that number for a suitable book. Have another look at *frame 183*.

Many of these requests come from readers who just wish to ' browse ' for ten minutes—perhaps before the start of a lesson or the departure of a bus. *Periodicals* are always useful for this —and up to date.

PTO FRAME 226

60 * Copy out this sentence on to your answer sheet, supplying the missing words:

'*Fiction* and *non-fiction*, books are, respectively, ——— and ———'

Remember that either kind of book may be *useful* and/or *entertaining* according to *your* purpose in choosing it.

PTO FRAME 61 TO CHECK ANSWER

---

143 This means that the books on our 'shelf' on *frame 128*, would be numbered, from left to right:

500, 510, 530 . . .

* Now you finish it off, using the details given on *frames 141 and 142*

PTO FRAME 144 TO CHECK ANSWER

---

226 Have a last look at the flow chart, then leave it and

PTO FRAME 227

61 The missing words were

    Untrue   and *true*

    Imaginative and *factual*

or any other pair of words conveying these two opposite ideas—
in this order!

If you were right, PTO *frame 62.* Otherwise

REVISE FRAMES 57-61

144 The full ' shelf ' should read:

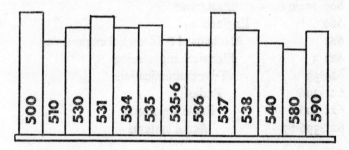

PTO FRAME 145

227 * *Now try to draw, on your answer sheet, the flow chart
which you have just been studying.*

Check and correct your copy as necessary after you have
finished and keep it handy in your notes as a quick

    ' *Guide to procedure in searching the library* '

Now PTO *frame 228* and we'll start on the last topic in this
programme.

62 Some of the books in a library may *not* be available for home-reading:

a) *Rare and other valuable books* must be safe-guarded for the benefit of the community. Most libraries have items that are *irreplaceable*.

PTO FRAME 63

---

145 Let's see how a really *long* decimal ' notation ' is built up:

600	main class TECHNOLOGIES
620	Engineering
621	Mechanical & Electrical engineering
621·3	Electrical engineering
621·39	Telecommunications
621·396	Radio
621·396·6	Radio apparatus
621·396·67	Aerial systems

PTO FRAME 146

---

228 Once the book is in your hands (*at last!*) don't assume that it is necessarily the best one for your purpose without closer examination.

Look at the following items which are included in nearly every book—but very seldom studied. They will help you to ' *assess* ' or ' *evaluate* ' the book:

PTO FRAME 229

63 b) Other books are designed, and kept in the Library, for reference purposes only.

It would be rather pointless to attempt to read straight through the library copy of an English *dictionary* at home—particularly if you only need to discover the meaning of a single word like ' incunabula '—you could write or telephone or call at the library in person and *refer* to this *reference book* in a matter of minutes.

PTO FRAME 64

---

146 In *this* particular ' family tree '—TECHNOLOGIES—we go down as far as the eighth generation.

' Aerial systems ' is the great-great-great-great-great grandson of old Joe Technology!

PTO FRAME 147

---

229 a) Examine the *title-page* to find:

i) *the full name and qualifications of the author* (not always clear from the spine of the book).

ii) *the full title of the book* which may include an *explanatory sub-title, eg New mathematics: for first year ONC students.*

iii) *the name of the publisher* who may, or may not, be well known and reliable.

PTO FRAME 230

3*

64 There are many other kinds of *reference book*.

Besides the *Dictionaries* already mentioned, of which there are several varieties, we have :

PTO FRAME 65

---

147 There are over 20,000 subject names in the latest *abridged* edition of one version of Dewey's decimal classification and their numbers run from 001 to 999, with decimal sub-divisions, of course.

This is the ' *Universal decimal classification* '.

It is widely used in technical libraries because it provides a relatively high proportion of places for scientific and technical subjects.

PTO FRAME 148

---

230 iv) On the *back of the title-page* is usually a statement about the *date of publication* of the book. It is usually important that a book should be up to date, especially in the fields of science and technology.

PTO FRAME 231

65—*Encyclopedias* (if you suspect that this is spelled incorrectly, check it in a *dictionary!*), *Trade directories, Telephone directories, Mathematical tables, Year books* and others—all designed to enable you to extract information quickly.

If you feel now that you ought to know more about these, read through *Frames 66-71.* Otherwise

PTO FRAME 72

---

148 *To summarize our ideas about the arrangement of books by their subjects:*

'It is agreed that it is generally most useful to readers to arrange books in libraries according to their *subjects,* using a *published classification* based on the idea of a '*family-tree*' *of subjects.* Thus books on subjects which are often studied together and form part of the same 'main class' of knowledge, are *located close together* on the library shelves and *identified by a code or* '*notation*', usually of numbers, printed on the books.'

PTO FRAME 149

---

231 v) Note in this connection that a statement of the *edition,* combined with the *date,* is a valuable guide. For example:

'*5th edition, 1967*' indicates that this is a very recent *revision of a popular and well-established book* which has been brought up to date with *new, more extensive and more accurate information* four times since it was first published.

PTO FRAME 232

66 i) An *Encyclopaedia* is like an expanded dictionary and may run to many volumes of fairly short articles, *covering between them practically every known subject* and laid out in a single *alphabetical arrangement of subject headings*:

Ammonia—Ammonite—Ammunition—Amnesia

Have a look at the *Encyclopaedia Britannica* next time you visit a library.

PTO FRAME 67

---

149 Look again at *frame 145* and notice how books on all these subjects would be usefully placed near together on the library shelves:

All the aspects of *Radio* are at—	621·396, *preceded by*:
other telecommunications at	621·39
electronics at	621·38
electrical engineering at	621·3 , *and followed by*:
television at	621·397
telecontrol and telemetering at	621·398

PTO FRAME 150

---

232 By contrast, the statement on the back of the title-page that this is the ' *5th impression* ' or ' *5th printing* 1967 ' means that there has probably been *no* change in the text since the first publication of the book—perhaps in *1867*!

Of course, a ' classic ' of literature, such as a novel by Dickens, a Shakespeare play or the poems of Keats, is not expected to be changed over the years—a radio book certainly *should* be changed!

PTO FRAME 233

67 ii) a *Trade directory* is a list of the important firms in a country or region. It will probably list them in alphabetical order by their names and then, perhaps, go on to list them again under the names of their various trades or products—'Ball-bearing manufacturers ', ' Cashmere de-hairers '.

A good example of this type of reference book is *Kelly's directory of manufacturers and merchants*.

PTO FRAME 68

---

150 On the shelves, the arrangement would look like this:

PTO FRAME 151

---

233 * Copy out these sentences on to your answer sheet, supplying the missing words:

' Somewhere on the t—— p—— of a book we can find the following information which helps us to ' assess ' or ' evaluate ' the book:

    i) A——'s n—— and q—— which help us to decide ——

_____

    ii) T—— of the book which should ——————————

_____

CONTINUED ON FRAME 234

68 iii) *Telephone directories*—look at the *directory in any public call box* and try to spot some of the many problems involved in arranging names in ' simple alphabetical order—for example, how does it arrange names beginning with the prefixes Mac, Mc, M'? How does it arrange all the entries beginning with the name of your town?

iv) *Mathematical tables*—ask to see a copy of *Four-figure mathematical tables* by Frank Castle.

PTO FRAME 69

---

151 With the appropriate number on the spine to ' describe ' its subject, a book can *quickly be found when requested* and *quickly returned to its proper place on the shelves after use.*

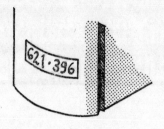

PTO FRAME 152

---

234 * iii) P——'s n——, which may help us to decide ——

iv) D—— of p——, which indicates ———————————

v) Statement of the e——, which may indicate ————

PTO FRAME 235 TO CHECK ANSWERS

69 v) *Year books* are of several different kinds—for example,

Whitaker's almanack contains general information about parliament, postal rates, duck-egg prices and a thousand other topics. It is revised every year and is extremely well indexed.

Year book of technical education and careers in industry, on the other hand, is a specialized account of one particular field of activity, again, revised every year and well indexed.

PTO FRAME 70

---

152 The code or ' *notation* ' may have special devices to simplify it or to make it easier to apply and remember.

For example, in the U—— D—— C—— scheme (*write the full name on your answer sheet):

a number in brackets indicates a country; (42) always means ' England '.

a number between inverted commas indicates a date; " 18 " always means the century 1800-1899.

PTO FRAME 153

---

235 Your answers should read : On *Title page* :

i) *Author's name and qualifications* help us to decide *whether or not the text is to be trusted.*

ii) *Title of the book* should *indicate its nature and purpose.*

iii) *Publisher's name* may help us to decide *whether or not the book is reliable and well-produced.*

iv) *Date of publication* indicates *whether or not the text is up-to-date.*

v) Statement of the *edition* should indicate *whether or not the book is popular and regularly revised.*

PTO FRAME 236

70 * Write down on your answer sheet your idea of the *kind* of r—— b—— represented by each of the following titles:

i) *Sell's directory of classified tr——s.*

ii) *Statesman's y—— b——.*

iii) British Academy: *Medieval latin word-list.*

iv) *Everyman's e——ia.*

v) Lindley, D V & Miller, J C P *Elementary Cambridge statistical t——s.*

PTO FRAME 71 TO CHECK ANSWERS

---

153 * What do you think would be an appropriate subject number for a book entitled:

Botany in England in the nineteenth century?

Look at *frames 141* and *152* for help and then

PTO FRAME 154 TO CHECK ANSWER

---

236 If your answers were substantially correct

PTO FRAME 237

If not—revise *frames 228-235* first.

71 Now check your answers about *reference books*:

i) *Trade directory*—listing firms alphabetically and by trades.

ii) *Year book*—describing all the countries of the world and their governments.

iii) *Dictionary*—'word-list', 'glossary' all mean approximately the same thing.

iv) *Encyclopaedia*—a small but very useful one.

v) *Mathematical tables* for statisticians.

Got those right? If so, PTO *frame 72*. If not, revise *frames 64-71* first.

Examine these books in a library.

---

154 An appropriate subject number might be:

580 (42) " 18 "

built up from:

580—Botany

(42)   in England

" 18 " (not " 19 ")   in the century 1800-1899

PTO FRAME 155

---

237 b) i) The *foreword* and/or *preface*: we sometimes find one or the other, sometimes both. These are written *by the author* to introduce himself and to explain his purpose in writing this book, on this subject, for this type of reader. The preface sometimes recounts briefly the outlines of the subject to which the book contributes.

PTO FRAME 238

72 *Librarians* can also help people to find and use certain *non-recorded communications*.

For example, local societies often organize *lectures, concerts, plays, and similar activities* and the local librarian may be asked to arrange these, advertise them and perhaps accommodate them in the library building which may thus become the *cultural centre of the district*.

PTO FRAME 73

---

155 Remember that certain kinds of books will usually be kept in *different rooms or on different sets of shelves* from the main collection.

For example : very large ' outsize ' books;
very valuable documents;
children's books;
reference books (*frames 63-71*);
pamphlets (usually kept in boxes).

These locations will be clearly marked in the various guides to the library and at the shelves.

PTO FRAME 156

---

238 ii) On the other hand, the *introduction* is usually by some person other than the author. It is nearly always very complimentary to the author (like the character-references which you enclose with your application for a job!) and unless the person who wrote the introduction is well known and trustworthy, it is as well to ignore it, or at least, read it critically!

PTO FRAME 239

73 *So much for libraries and their contents in general terms.*
It is important to remember that there are
Different types of library for
　Different groups of people and for
　Different purposes.

PTO FRAME 74

---

156 Remember also that *alphabetical order,* for example, by names of authors, can still be useful in certain circumstances, for the further arrangement of books once they are sorted into subject order:

Once we have isolated all the books on 'Colour' and numbered them '535·6', we may have so many that it is desirable to sub-divide the group alphabetically by the authors' names. We should then distinguish 535·6 Adams, 535·6 Brown, 535·6 Craven and may even add the initials to the subject number.

PTO FRAME 157

---

239 c) The exact '*coverage*' of the book within its subject field and the amount of detail in its treatment may be found by a quick glance through:

　i) *Contents list*
　ii) *Index*
　iii) *Illustrations list*
　iv) *Glossary or vocabulary*

These serve as a useful check on the author's statements in his preface and/or foreword.

PTO FRAME 240

74 a) *Public libraries* are to be found in nearly every country in the world. In Britain they are provided by the borough, urban district and county councils, financed from the rates paid by all householders, and used by about one third of the population.

'Lending departments' cater for 'general' reading needs, mainly novels and popular non-fiction books, together with a number of more serious volumes on current social and scientific problems, handicrafts and so on.

PTO FRAME 75

---

157 Again—*novels* often form one third of the stock of a large library and two thirds of the total of books issued. Readers usually have favourite authors and ask for *these* books by the authors' names (see *frame 120*).

So it is sensible to arrange *novels* alphabetically by the authors' names, either at the appropriate subject number on the shelves— 823—, or perhaps on separate shelves altogether.

PTO FRAME 158

---

240 For example:

the book may be entitled *Radio service training manual,* but only by looking at the *contents list* and *index* could you find out whether or not it covers the servicing of mobile and vehicle-borne equipment.

PTO FRAME 241

75 Public libraries reach readers in the *suburbs and countryside* through *branch libraries* and *travelling library vehicles.*

They serve *special groups* of *hospital patients, school children, teachers, blind* and *house-bound* people, with general reading books.

They have *special departments* for *reference books, local history documents, patent specifications, music recordings, and other media of communication.*

PTO FRAME 76

---

158 However, the *arrangement of names in ' simple ' alphabetical order,* on library shelves, in a card index or on a list of any other kind, *raises a surprising number of difficulties.*

The American Library Association has devised 152 rules for this alone!

But there are *four* common difficulties :

PTO FRAME 159

---

241 d) a guide to further reading on the same subject or allied subjects, and a clue as to where your author gathered the information for his book, may be found in the

Reading lists, ' bibliographies ' or ' references ' of books and periodical articles which are often placed at the end of the book or at the ends of the individual chapters.

PTO FRAME 242

76 * Write down on your answer sheet:

i) The location of your nearest public library service point.

ii) The name and address of the local authority which runs it.

iii) The cost of joining and using it.

iv) Three important library functions which you would expect to find in the building.

PTO FRAME 77

---

159 a) We must decide whether to arrange names

i) '*Word-by-word* as though terms 1 & 2 consisted of the one word 'New' only
  1 New Hampshire
  2 New York
  3 Newark
  4 Newtown.

ii) '*Letter-by-letter*', ignoring the fact that terms 2 & 4 have two separate words:
  1 Newark
  2 New Hampshire
  3 Newtown
  4 New York

PTO FRAME 160

---

242 'Bibliographies' should really be complete and fully comprehensive lists of the books or articles published in a given country and/or period, on a given subject, or by a given writer (if in doubt have another look at *frames 204-210*).

However, this term is sometimes used to mean selective 'reading lists' as described on *frame 241*, and is also used in this sense in catalogue entries (*frame 187*).

PTO FRAME 243

77 i) } *We* don't know the answers to these questions because
ii) we don't know where you live—but if *you* don't know
iii) the answers, it might be a good idea to find out. In
any case there should be no charge for joining or using the
library.

iv) However small this service point may be it should have
a lending library for adults, another one for children and a
collection of reference books.

PTO FRAME 78

---

160 b) We must also decide how to arrange ' *double-barrelled* '
names. For example:
i) SMITH-DAVIES, William *or*
ii) -DAVIES, William SMITH- ?
The *former way is usually preferred,* but we try to respect
the author's wishes and usage. Beware of names that are *not*
really ' double-barelled '—MAUGHAM, William Somerset.

PTO FRAME 161

---

243 * Copy the following sentences on to your answer sheet,
supplying the missing words:
i) The F—— and/or P—— give the author an opportunity
to explain his p——s and q——s.

ii) C—— l—— and I—— help the reader to estimate the
book's c—— of its subject field.

PTO FRAME 244 TO CHECK ANSWER

78 b) *National libraries* are designed to serve the country as a whole, or its government; for example:

i) *The British Museum* has the colossal task of preserving at least one copy of every book published in this country. At present, the rate of 'legal deposit' is about 25,000 books each year.

The 'BM' also has many invaluable newspaper files and a huge collection of antique and foreign books.

PTO FRAME 79

---

161 c) *Noblemen, married women,* and some other people *change their names during their working life.* Would you arrange this writer's books on electricity under:

THOMSON, William   *or* his later title:

KELVIN, William Thomson, 1st Baron?

Generally, we would prefer to put all his books together under the *later and better-known name.*

PTO FRAME 162

---

244 The sentences should read:

i) The *Foreword* and/or *Preface* give the author an opportunity to explain his *purposes* and *qualifications.*

ii) *Contents list* and *index* help the reader to estimate the book's *coverage* of its subject field.

PTO FRAME 245

79 ii) On the other hand, the *National Lending Library for Science and Technology* (NLLST), specializes in a speedy postal service for the loan of modern *scientific and technical periodicals* of many countries.

A *translation service* is available and, if you prefer, you can buy cheap *photographic copies* of the articles you need.

PTO FRAME 80

---

162 d) Many *organizations* produce books :

i) *Government publications* could be brought together under the name of the country :

UNITED STATES : Defense Department.

British ministries and departments may have their publications arranged *directly* under their name :

MINISTRY OF AGRICULTURE, FISHERIES & FOOD

or, better still, under the ' key-word ' :

AGRICULTURE, FISHERIES & FOOD, MINISTRY OF.

PTO FRAME 163

---

245 * ' ——— ', ' ——— ', ' ——— ' are three names given to items in many books which are guides to further reading and to the sources of the author's ideas.

Supply the missing words on your answer sheet.

PTO FRAME 246 TO CHECK ANSWER

80 iii) *Government departments* have their own library services: the Ministry of Agriculture, Fisheries & Food, Department of Education & Science, Board of Trade, and most of the others. The House of Commons has a library to serve the information needs of its members. These are not usually open directly to the public but help to ensure efficient operation of the departments for the public good.

PTO FRAME 81

---

163 ii) *Societies and institutions* can be regarded as authors of their publications, too. These are, perhaps, best arranged under their usually accepted names:

ASSOC SOC OF LOCOMOTIVE ENGINEERS & FIREMEN

INST OF ELECTRICAL ENGINEERS

INST OF MECHANICAL ENGINEERS.

Notice how useful it is to abbreviate words which are often confused—ASSOCIATED/ASSOCIATION, INSTITUTE/INSTITUTION.

PTO FRAME 164

---

246 Did you think that we had forgotten about:

' *Reading lists* ', ' *References* ', ' *Bibliographies* '?

These guide the reader to further reading and to the sources of the author's ideas.

PTO FRAME 247

81 * Can you name two important tasks that should be allocated to a newly organized
' *National library* '?
Write your suggestions on your answer sheet and head them
' National libraries '.

PTO FRAME 82 TO CHECK ANSWERS

---

164 iii) The use of *initials* is widespread, but do we arrange publications by
UNITED NATIONS EDUCATIONAL SCIENTIFIC & CULTURAL ORGANIZATION under
U.N.E.S.C.O. as an abbreviation at the beginning of the ' U ' section, *or*
UNESCO as a word coming between UNERI and UNILEVER, *or*
U.N.E.S.C.O. at the place it would occupy if spelled out in full?
This latter method is often preferred.

PTO FRAME 165

---

247 To end on a rather less technical note—*don't be afraid to judge a book, at least in part, by its appearance*—the strength of its boards, cloth and *binding;* the quality and texture of the *paper;* the clarity and style of the *print* and *illustrations,* and the care with which the items mentioned in *frames 228-246* have been prepared.

PTO FRAME 248

82 Tasks for a newly-organized '*National Library*' might include:

i) Collecting copies of all books published in the country or all the useful books in a particular wide subject field.

ii) Collecting all important foreign books.

iii) Collecting important newspapers and periodicals.

iv) Setting up a photographic copying service to deal with enquiries for information.

If you didn't get *any* of these answers, revise *frames 78-80*. When you are satisfied, *please turn back to frame 83 which you will find in the centre section of page 9.*

---

165 * On your answer sheet, try to arrange the following names in *alphabetical order,* according to the recommendations on *frames 159-164:*

1 Willys, *Sir* Edmund 2 Saint Patrick 3 Gwynn-Williams, D 4 Wright, Barbara, 1st Baroness Wootton of Abinger 5 Ministry of Technology of Great Britain 6 Saintbury, H 7 Association of Scottish Secondary Teachers 8 WHO (World Health Organization) 9 Associated Metalworkers' Society.

To check your answers, *please turn back to frame 166 which you will find in the lower section of page 9.*

---

248 There are no more summary frames—your completed answer sheets should summarize the whole book and serve to refresh your memory as necessary—if necessary!

For a list of further reading, the index to this book and specimen answers, turn to pages 94, 95 and 100 respectively.

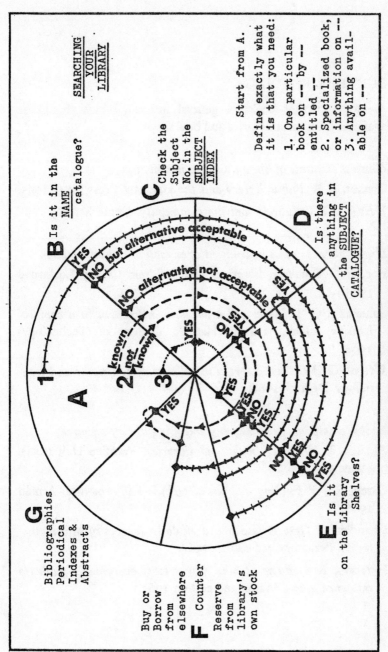

FLOW CHART: SEARCHING YOUR LIBRARY

SEARCHING YOUR LIBRARY

Start from A.

Define exactly what it is that you need:

1. One particular book on — by — entitled —
2. Specialized book, or information on —
3. Anything available on —

C Check the Subject No. in the SUBJECT INDEX

B Is it in the NAME catalogue?

D Is there anything in the SUBJECT CATALOGUE?

YES
NO but alternative acceptable
NO alternative not acceptable

known
not known

A
1
2
3

YES
NO
YES

YES
YES
NO
YES
YES
NO
YES
NO
YES

G
Bibliographies
Periodical
Indexes &
Abstracts

Buy or
Borrow
from
elsewhere

F Counter

Reserve
from
library's
own stock

E Is it
on the Library
Shelves?

93

FURTHER READING

A SHORT LIST of books of general interest, which should be available from most libraries and bookshops.

General accounts of library services in daily life
Conant, R W *Public library and the city*. MIT Press (USA) 1965.
Harrison, K C *Library and the community*. Deutsch 1963.

Use of libraries as an instrument of education and information
Roe, E C *Teachers, librarians and children*. Crosby Lockwood 1965.
Salusburg, G T *Library as a teaching instrument in a comprehensive school*. HERTIS (Hatfield College of Technology) 1968.
Wright, G H (editor) *Library in colleges of commerce and technology*. Deutsch 1966.

Books to help you in identifying and using library resources
Aldrich, E V *Using books and libraries*. Prentice Hall (USA). 5th edition 1967.
Carey, R J P *Finding and using technical information*. Arnold 1966.
Chandler, G *How to find out, a guide to sources of information for all*. Pergamon 3rd edition 1968.
Harrison, K C *Facts at your finger tips, everyman's guide to reference books*. Mason 2nd edition 1967.

INDEX

SPECIMEN ANSWER SHEETS AND REVISION OUTLINE

frame no

1 Communication—the art & science of passing knowledge.

8 Without communication, we could not therefore—govern, educate, develop art science technology, maintain friendly relations, cumulate knowledge.

14 Communication is the art & science of passing knowledge.

Literacy is the ability to read & write, to absorb knowledge and use it to solve personal and social problems.

Communication media are the items of equipment & the actual words & illustrations used to pass knowledge between people.

17 Communication: Literacy: Communication media.

20 Communication media:

a) Brief & transient: Television programmes, conversations, films & plays, records & tapes, periodicals & newspapers, radio programmes, paintings & drawings, sculptures, lectures.

b) More comprehensive & lasting: Books.

25 Books are usually comprehensive, permanent, cheap, convenient.

Books can be illustrated, supplemented, up-dated, analysed.

27 People without good communications: Australian aborigines, Red Indians, Stone Age men, Tibetans, Hottentots (from SW Africa).

30 The name given to the process by which people can be made literate is Education.

35 Media used for socialization, instruction, entertainment, expression, research.

40 ' Literacy is the ability to use communication media for receiving & passing on to others, communications & knowledge. We acquire this ability through the process of education and must learn to use it at various stages of our life for purposes of socialization, instruction, entertainment, expression & research. Perhaps the most important medium to the truly literate person is the book.'

frame no

52 Librarians are people who select, store, display & deploy books & other media of communication. Librarians should also try to help & train their readers to become efficient library users.

53 This particular programme is intended to help & train you to become an efficient library user; to teach you how to:
a) state your needs in 'library language'; b) carry out, by yourself, in the library, the first stages of the search for what you need.

60 Fiction and non-fiction books are respectively untrue & true—imaginative & factual ...

70 Reference books—Trade directory, Year book, Dictionary, Encyclopaedia, Mathematical tables.

76 i) Public library; ... County branch library etc;
ii) ... County borough council; ... County council etc.
iii) There should be no charge.
iv) Lending libraries for adults & children & a collection of reference books.

81 National library:
i) Collecting copies of all books published in the country or all the useful books in a particular wide subject field.
ii) Collecting all important foreign books.
iii) Collecting important newspapers & periodicals.
iv) Setting up a photographic copying service to deal with enquiries for information.

84 Special libraries:
i) National film library—to stock a special kind of communication medium—film.
ii) College libraries in general—for a special kind of reader—students & teachers.
iii) *Your* college library—for a particular group of readers in *your* college.
iv) Science museum library—to cover a special subject—science.

88 i) File of *The times* for 1801: National library (British Museum).

ii) Latest novel by Muriel Spark: local public library lending dept.

iii) Latest Ministry of Agriculture, Fisheries & Food pamphlet on fowl pest: local public library reference dept.

iv) Last July's issue of a Japanese textile periodical: National Lending Library for Science & Technology.

v) Very dull nineteenth century book of sermons: National library (British Museum).

vi) Copy of an early Charlie Chaplin film: National Film Library.

vii) Latest edition of *Radio handbook* by William Orr: Your college library or local public library lending or reference dept.

91 Select, store, display, deploy.

92 Cooperate.

94 Summary of part 2: 'Librarians are people who select, store, display & deploy books & other communication media in libraries. They also help & train library users. Books, fiction & non-fiction, for lending & reference, are made available through public, national & special libraries which cooperate with each other to serve readers.'

Part 3: How libraries work

100 Surname, forenames, admission no, address, course, date, signature.

102 Name in full, address, age if under 21, date, signature, business or school address if not living locally; guarantor's name in full, address & signature.

108 i) People should give full & correct details when filling in application-for-membership forms.

ii) They should not take out books to which they are not entitled, or more books than allowed.

iii) They should return books on or before the due date.

iv) They should report any change of home address.

v) They should report any case of infectious disease at home.

vi) They should never disturb or offend other readers.

115 Should you ask a library assistant to:

a) Show you how to fill in the application-for-membership form? Yes—but the librarian should make his forms easy to fill in.

b) Show you how to find the books on radio servicing? Yes, but she should show you the guide which helps you to locate books on all subjects rather than just lead you to the radio books on the shelves.

c) Order five very expensive books on radio servicing for the library stock? No—the librarian is responsible for book selection.

d) Change the library rules about the length of time you can keep a book? No, even the librarian would consult the library committee about changing the rules.

119 We could arrange books by author's name, by size, by colour, by title.

120 We must arrange books by their subjects.

127 All the sciences, Maths, Physics, Mechanics, Sound, Light, Colour, Heat, Electricity, Magnetism, Chemistry, Botany, Zoology.

135 Encyclopaedias go in the GENERAL BOOKS class.

136	000	GENERAL BOOKS	500	SCIENCES
&	100	PHILOSOPHY	600	TECHNOLOGIES
139	200	RELIGION	700	ARTS
	300	SOCIAL STUDIES	800	LITERATURES
	400	LANGUAGES	900	HISTORY & GEOGRAPHY

143 500, 510, 530, 531, 534, 535, 535·6, 536, 537, 538, 540, 580, 590.

152 Universal decimal classification.

153 580 (42) " 18 " ' Botany in England in the 19th century '.

165 1 Assoc Metalworkers' Soc

2 Assoc (of) Scottish Secondary Teachers

3 Gwynn-Williams, D

165 4 Saint Patrick
    5 Saintbury, H
    6 Technology, Min of
    7 Willys, *Sir* Edmund
    8 Wootton of Abinger, Barbara Wright, 1st Baroness
    9 WHO

Part 4: How to use books & libraries

167 Summary of part 3: 'Most libraries ask new readers to complete an application-for-membership form. They agree to keep the simple rules for the convenience of the other library users. Library assistants record & control the loan of books. An arrangement of books by their subjects is most useful to a majority of readers and this is achieved by the use of a special classification & its associated notation.'

175 Index.

177 Subject index.

189 Index, subjects, alphabetical, page numbers. Subject index, subjects, shelves, notation.

190 Subject catalogue. 'Entries are arranged in the same subject order as are the books on the shelves.'

i) 'A complete & easily accessible inventory of the library's resources on any subject.'

ii) 'A list of the items which are not on the shelves when we visit the library.'

192

940

    SOUTHGATE, George W

        Shorter European History 1756-1943
        Dent, 1944

        285 p.

---

200 Name catalogue, author, illustrator, sponsor, editor, title, series.

209 'Periodical indexes & periodical abstracts list important magazine articles, usually in subject order, at monthly or quarterly intervals. On the other hand, bibliographies list books published in a given country &/or period or on a given subject or by a given author.'

213 Subject index, subject catalogue, name catalogue, bibliographies, periodical indexes & abstracts.

227 [Reproduction of flow chart on page 93.]

233/4 On title page:

i) Author's name & qualifications help us to decide whether or not the text is to be trusted.

ii) Title of the book should indicate its nature & purpose.

iii) Publisher's name may help us to decide whether or not the book is reliable & well-produced.

iv) Date of publication indicates whether or not the text is up to date.

v) Statement of the edition should indicate whether or not the book is popular & regularly revised.

243 i) Foreword and/or preface give the author an opportunity to explain his purposes & qualifications.

ii) Contents list & index help the reader to estimate the book's coverage of its subject field.

245 Reading lists, references, bibliographies.